CAMBRIC POETRY PROJECT ONE

edited by

JOEL RUDINGER

Cambric Press
912 Strowbridge
Huron, Ohio 44839

Copyright © 1978, by Cambric Press

Front Cover Art, Robin Shell

All rights reserved. No part of this book may be reproduced in any form without written permission from the publisher. Manufactured in the United States of America.

First printing November 1978

CONTENTS

Chris Agar	48	Susan Landgraf	108
JoAnn Amadeo	15	Ruth Laney	105
Nova Trimble Ashley	7	Lance Lee	102
Jim Barry	37	Linda Lerner	29
Guy R. Beining	20	Judith Lindenau	58
Benjamin Scott Blake	16	Norman Lock	66
F. Anthony Blankenship	60	Manna Lowenfels-Perpelitt	105
Lucile Bogue	21	Mike Lowery	52
Danny M. Bounds	39	Ron McFarland	65
Terry W. Brown	41	Jesse McKnight	73
Martin Burwell	40	David L. Meth	59
Marilyn Carmen	27	Frank Moore	13
Melissa Clark	26	Gudrun Mouw	74
John Warwick Daniel III	94	Mary-Ruth Mundy	76
Robert Dunn	47	Jennifer Nostrand	88
Esther Erford	35	Charles V. Olynyk	90
Gail Festa	100	Karolyn Pettingell	62
Kathleen Gillette	57	Kevin Pilkington	64
Michael S. Glaser	107	Susan Irene Rea	17
Glenna Glee	92	Harland Ristau	89
Frances M. Greene	32	Larry Rochelle	93
Nickie Gunstrom	60	John Roth	42
Carl Scott Harker	65	Salvatore Salerno, Jr.	50
Janet Ruth Heller	68	Ruth Wildes Schuler	38
Thomas Hickenbottom	72	Rennis H. Sees	67
David Holdt	18	Ruby R. Shackleford	28
E. Manuel Huber	91	C. A. Smith	107
Philip Hughes	54	Jared Smith	71
Dwight E. Humphries	44	Laurel Speer	30
Joe C. Ireland	92	Gary Sterling	75
Phillis Janowitz	59	Ronica Stern	90
Anthony C. Kallas	97	Deborah Stevens	103
Hannah Kahn	96	Nancy Stone	93
Bob Kaplan	64	Robert Joe Stout	49
Binnie Klein	95	John Thomas Stovall	89
Ian Krieger	70	Eileen Stratidakis	106
Venkatesh Srinivas Kulkarni	8	Robert J. Svoboda	69

Melissa Szymanski	53
Marcella Taylor	22
J. Maurice Thomas	34
Scott Thomas	101
June W. Thornton	55
Marilyn Throne	88
WDTimmerman	91
Rick Ulman	63
Charles Upton	61
David Vadja	45
Lois V. Walker	98
The Walrus	24
David Wann	68
Robert R. Ward	31
Roger Weaver	74
Randy Weinstein	51
W. Blaine Wheeler	14
Robert F. Whisler	23
William M. White	46
Doris Wight	99
Kim Williamson	63
Robert L. Wilson	73
Liz Wrenn	75
About the Contributors	109
Index to the Poems	119

CAMBRIC
POETRY PROJECT
ONE

STAR GATHERER

I straddle the dream horse
of imagination;
his nostrils dilate,
his white wings,
my dark cloak and hair,
caress the clouds.
Muscle rippling on muscle
I ride, clutching
the angel-silk mane
no reins to guide,
for who would steer
this ethereal being
in wandering Fantasy?
Enraptured, I ignore
the compass of direction.
Let Pegasus find his way.
Delirium of being lost
in Musing
countervanes the pain
of Reality.

                          Nova Trimble Ashley

SUSAN IN NEWCASTLE

> To Radheshyam Sharma and
> Randolph Bates— the Poem
> and the Persons in a Harmony of three cultures

smartly dressed
in a dark, beige suit
probably a resident of the flats
close to the bridge
near the Newcastle railway station
seedy and inappropriate
she comes to say goodbye
to her lover
a soldier
ready to fight
Catholics and Protestants
alike in Londonderry
a man, like me,
ready to make the journey
beyond the Hebrides
beyond Aberdeen and Inverness
beyond all the places
where they make vintage Scotch
beyond the place
where the ancient mariner's albatross
was sighted

sharp as the salt air
of the city
she kisses her boyfriend
passionately
The soldier
in a quiet, military movement
slides his hand under her skirt
and I sense her flooding
like little Tweed under Berwick
submerging her loneliness
in the tenderness of his palm

the *others* smile helplessly
like polite English sheep
and pretend indifference
to what they dare not
acknowledge

the train arrives
steaming in
people rush, and scramble,
and forget, and board the train
but it is she
who came to say goodbye,
as I had imagined,
boards the train
to my surprise
and leaves her soldier
behind

now I cannot leave my emotions
behind
and ruminate about the dark, rich,
luscious forest around her vagina
she brings the dream with her
carrying coals away from Newcastle!

I imagine
I have seen her before
but I have felt that way
about every beautiful girl
I ever met from Prague
to Passaic, New Jersey
How could I
have ever known intimately
a girl
who reads Gray's *Anatomy*
so intensely!

I imagine
I still see her soldier
poor fellow

listening to the distant whistle
from the Scottish highlands
as he is surrounded
by sandwich vendors
and gentlemen
reading *The Manchester Guardian*
There's no news for him
in that!

I feel sympathetic for him
as the train arrives in Edinburgh

I feel I have known
the strange, dim lights
somewhere in the past
The railway station
The hansom cabs
The Scottish melodies!

The girl alights
and is met
by a seven year old
Scottish lassie
a veritable princess
bewitching
in her beauty
carrying flowers
for her mother
my past companion
the woman from Newcastle
runs to embrace the girl
on the platform

and
they crush the flowers
together

I look
at the little girl

I remember
the lily-blossoms
of East Anglia

I climb the Tower
of King's College
and stare
into the vast hinterland
of Cambridge

The mother cries "Susan."
I know Susan now
Not the little girl
but the grown woman
whose vagina
the soldier had craved
with such urgency
in Newcastle
That's my Susan
making gentle truce
with my daughter
Susan

Should I carry her
beyond Aberdeen
Or go there myself?

The ancient castle
above me
is not lighted
What bus do they wish
to take in Scotland?

Shall I follow them
or catch the train
back to Newcastle
to meet the soldier
my rival and companion?

Under the biting, cold
northern discomfort
of Scotland
sunlight
blazes brilliantly

There is no train here
Susan is in Scotland
And Newcastle is miles away.

***

dimpled
with sparkling brown eyes
and dug-in breasts

in multiple plaids

laughingly concealing
their mountain-dew'd
pubescent desires
they parade themselves

under the biting, cool,
northern discomfort
of the Scottish moonlight

the ancient castles
bright and dark
lonely and romantic
sparkle
at the same instant
of chiaroscuro
and Princess Street
is lit
like a Christmas tree.

Ventakesh Srinivas Kulkarni

THE VISIT

A decade ago I drove this road
winding through trees in Kentucky.
My hands were wet on the wheel
when I parked below the house.
I could see you pacing on the proch,
the faded hat shading your brow
and the grin you saved for visits.
We touched as we entered the door:
a brush of skin that burned me,
a reminder of the night your wiry
body ran at me again and again,
until I held you off with a gun.
So, a table between us, we pulled
at words like strangers who must
wait too long in the same room.
The apple pie was metal in my mouth.

Now, driving again to you, daisies
from Philadelphia arriving before me,
I see your face propped on a pillow,
feel your hands like wax under mine.
I rehearse the word Father one more time.

Frank D. Moore

MEMORY OF A FAMILY

You are just over the hilltop
where the sun fades past the trees.
They wave like a curtain hiding
another slope and the farm below.
I am in front sliding on gravel;
I can feel your smiles on my neck.
As we near the path in the wood,
you walk together, arms touching,
closer than the white shapes who

stay in the frame on the mantel.
We pass under the roof of leaves,
head downhill for the last time.

                Frank D. Moore

The auction flyer said there were items
Too numerous to mention in addition
                to all those listed.
I guess that's right. How would
Memories of a sick baby with no
Money for a doctor be mentioned?
Or the elation of a son's high school
Diploma, the first in the family?
When the old house is finally emptied
                and all the buyers
              and the auctioneer
              have left,
I think there will still be items
Too numerous to mention.

                W. Blaine Wheeler

QUIET...

i lay here
quiet
in your arms
in this complicated world
that makes me sometimes
scream inside!

lightning passes between us
                        as usual...

it always does you know.

yet,
you
understand me
well enough my love

to just
brush away my unseen tears,
wrap yourself tightly
around my pain
and gently
kiss away the night...

                        JoAnn Amadeo

CALLING CAPTAIN CLIVE

This is the third night this summer
That I've sat at this desk
Thinking about you driving through Europe
With Ruth and your beard
Living more in July
Than I have in ten Julys
Finding out
(But I can only guess)
That home can be far away
And not be lonely
That home can disappear
And not be sad
That love is as long as the road
And the gas
As long as summer

Remember cousin Bob?
I have the word he's getting married
The same Bob, but not the same
Who almost croaked when I got married
Who thought it was the end of everything
Who shook my hand like I was going to the stars

We've changed
All of us have changed
All us summer-in-Maine
Babies
Children
Adolescents
All us cousins
All us friends

Baseball lives
Hoss Cartwright dies
The world still lets me ride
While you ride Ruth
And the rolling road

And since you can't be pegged by telephone
Or chained by general delivery
I must now give this to the native runner
Who will give it to the native drummer
Who will give it to the wind

                        Benjamin Scott Blake

DAUGHTER AT TEN

Thin breezes move in these fields, invisible,
Menacing as the changes that begin in me,
The blind blood moving toward its start,
The buds that will crest and blossom, mountaining
Into womanhood. No-one has asked me
If I want that. I see how the earth, at heart,
Is cold and puddled beneath these drying
November weeds. Childhood is a fable.

Soon I will be my mother, so unyieldingly
Life has made me. Home is already gone, perhaps.
A thin, invisible smoke drifts
This way. Here a stump bends like an old man;
If I touch him, bark will break off in my hand.
Insects mottle it like sparks; wood turns to ash.
The flames cut me off, flaring rifts.
Oh, fire, I bury myself in the cool mud and weep.

                        Susan Irene Rea

GRAVITY

It is good to see my dog
running in the woods
free and clear of chains
between her and the trees.
No mud of the realities
of that circle without grass
she has paced and over-passed
in exhausting possibilities.
She's stretching now, at last.

No crowded rooms of furniture
will curb her wagging spirit
for she's sniffing up on dreams
from some early incarnation
and flagging her elation
with her tail. Still

she circles in her flying
and of her own volition
she is centering.
Her radius is not leash-held
yet there is gravity
in her positioning.
And she orbits
and I orbit
down the trail.

David Holdt

DOVES

Under the bank of the pond
tawny gray and pink against
the snow and yellow reeds
three mourning doves were
resting, nesting nearby I
suppose.
I came upon them quietly
on whisking skis;
they did not start to fly
until I was quite near.
To hear them whistle up
in fright and see how clumsily
they fight for altitude
was nothing new.
But later, when they circled
back, and I was farther
down the track they
whispered past
like arrowed ghosts
flying so fast
I almost knew they
were.

                        David Holdt

keeping up with weather & politics

i ride my bike along the grasslands
of my dream
i ride around a well
butterflies follow me
as silken gowns
i ride on the splash of water
up over ginger spokes of sunlight
the pedals liquefy
i am treading water
the sky is under me
i eat the smoke of steam
curtains rise and fall
there is merriment in the colony of nature
finally i ride up my sleeve
& disappear into the dark blotch
of blood
chinese red & perfectly round.

Guy R. Beining

TO A YOUNG BALLET DANCER
(In Memoriam)

A flame
Soft and tender
As a candle
Lit at night
To warm the heart

Battered
By such tempests
As would quench
A lesser light
The flame burns on

Courage
Of the mountain ash
In autumn storm
And just as bright...
A steady fire

The ring
Of warmth is wide
Enough to touch
A thousand nights
With humble beauty

This flame
In giving joy
Is quietly devoured...
But dear delight...
We are the richer

                              Lucile Bogue

ORDAINED ACTS

In preparation for the city
I trim my hair, collect the pieces
take their shadows with me

I climb six flights
a building brown and worn

An old friend greets me
lanky, graceful, he smiles
leads me into three rooms
all opened into each other

Outside the rain does not fall
but there is no drought
The bronze cross-legged buddha
bows. I pass him
what is left of the setting sun

My hair begins to grow quickly
as I wait for each bus
    under a city moon
when I lean over the telephone
    strands are caught in filigree branches

The day I pass the sign of a palmist
I reverse direction
A narrow stair greets me
a dark door   a knocker
No one emerges

I smile
Travelling light
I return to the buddha
wait for the rain and another sunset

                        Marcella Taylor

TO A NUN/STANDING ON THE SHORE

Are you, then, the nun on the shore,
or the sea that unearths earth
where you stand too timid to explore
its timeless tidal sweep? Love's birth
and death in unending waves break
beneath your feet, wash ashore
like an empty shell or disjointed bone
but return to you none of your own
where you wait — what,
the woman you were before?

                              Robert F. Whisler

MUSICAL DRAINS

All in a row the musical drains
ring to the rain's dull drone
drumming, drumming down —
and I all alone and half asleep am slow
to keep time to the weather's watery tempo
dripping, dripping down —
down to the pool's deep dreamy plash
where the pipes' patter and the roof's splatter
splash and quietly drown.

                              Robert F. Whisler

FROM THE NEST

She said, "Why don't you just forget her?
She'll be the death of you.
Even if you get her
You know she won't be true.
She'll just run off with other men
Who'll use her as they will,
And then she will come back again
And foot you with the bill."

I said, "Mama, I love her.
Why can't you understand?
I love you, too, Mother,
But now I am a man.
I'll do anything to keep her here
Where I will know she's mine;
Cause I know if I keep her near
She'll love me all the time."

She said, "Don't be so foolish—
She's a tramp with curls and lies;
I know you're being mulish
Just to cut me down to size.
But I am your mother;
I know you very well;
I know that you don't love her—"
I said, "Mother please don't yell."

I said, "You know I'll marry her
If she comes back to me;
You know I want to carry her—
To make her my queen bee.
You're just afraid to let me go—
To break me from the nest;
That is why you must say 'No'—
Now *that* you must confess."

She said, "You know I'm not that way.
I want the best for you.

I know that every word you say
Comes right out of the blue.
You know I love you very much
And want you to be free.
I just don't want that such-and-such
Make you too blind to see."

I said, "Mother, you're lonely;
All you've got is me.
I'm your one and only
But you've got to set me free.
You know I love you, Mother,
But I've got to live my life;
I just tell you I love her
And I want to make her wife."

She said, "I'm old and invalid—
I need you home with me,
And not a fool for that young kid
For all the world to see.
I need you here to give me care—
To put me into bed—
To put me into my wheelchair
And keep me well," she said.

I said, "I will get someone
To work for you instead.
You know I'm not a wicked man
Who'd make you stay in bed."
I said, "You won't be lonely
Cause we'll be stopping by,
Cause I'm your one and only."
Then she began to cry.

She said, "Why don't you forget her?
She'll be the death of you.
Even if you get her
You know she won't be true.
She'll just run off with other men
Who'll use her as they will,

25

And then she will come back again
And foot you with the bill."

I said, "Mama, I love her....

> The Walrus

> resurrectionist

unearth me   lover
i'm a jewel now   melted
in that crevice that you loved so
well   it's a socket now an
ingot   for my mingled liquid
essence   come and suck it up
dust lathered lips
strip   the flesh as you once
did the clothes   i'm burning
cinder hot for you   let
me astound you with
my death perfected skill

> Melissa Clark

"MANOR" BESIDE FIERY "BROOKS" OF HELL

It's so nice
to walk
though "The Manor"

No stones
are thrown
at me

No rope
is waiting
for my neck

Only green grass
Dotted flowers
Little white kids swimming
   while mine watch TV

Manager said "Stay home," you see

His manner is kind
like that of "The Manor"

   three-piece suit
   velvet socks

It's so nice
to walk
through "The Manor"

                       Marilyn Carmen

SONNET VII

If I had owned what has been yours
And through neglect had lost the claim,
I'd move among the soulless throng
And drop my head to hide the shame.
If I had held that high esteem
So rare to find, so wide acclaimed,
No love of mirth nor press of time
Would lay the ground for my self-blame.
If I had found that changeless faith
A trust complete, strength adamant
No urge, nor need, however great,
Could have usurped that governance.
Such heavenly gifts, by grace attained,
When lost, leave life a futile plain.

       Ruby P. Shackleford

AVOIDANCE

The avoidance is all.
We corner our love
like a wounded animal,
its appearance so untimely

we withhold
gesture after gesture, quicker
than hunters with their slings.

Afterwards we forget.
A smile passes between us
like a stray deer and disappears
before we remember.

in dreams, a mirror grows
blossoming odd reflections,

the room of expensive furniture,
crimson drapes, silver cupids
climbing gold borders;
the air is full of arrows.

We are there, sitting
statue-stiff and as white,
our backs to each other.
On the table is a cup of tea
carved from bone.

Slowly, we face each other
and drink our way out
of this reflection.

      Linda Lerner

TERMINATE

If we could think
Of another word
For abortion
Of unwanted births,
Of babies conceived
In heroin rushes
Or after the fifth pint
Of Ripple,
Or under the itch
Of syphilitic sores
So the twisted bodies
That monster down the birth canal
Could end
Before they began.

No legislator
Has to live with a wart
On his organ
From voting no.

A word that could skirt the voters,
Absolve senators
From staring helplessly
At enraged, barren parents
Passed over as unfit
For adoption.
A word like
Terminate?

Laurel Speer

WHY DON'T YOU FEEL ANYTHING WHEN I TOUCH YOU THERE

You call on St Sylvia of the Oven,
voice grainy as a curlew's cry;
your glance implying knuckles whitened
around the handle of a flint-bladed sickle.

We circle one another, stifflegged as strange
dogs smelling for submission, certain
that blood is less bitter than
the soft convention of tears.

Your clothes are too tight for your anger,
you fear the supple rigidity of your nipples;
you snarl, the white rhythm of your teeth clashing
as you publicly bare your wounds.

There is no denying the ecstasy of your bitterness,
sister hate is closer than blood;
must I too fall sacrifice
under the razor of your rage?

                          Robert R. Ward

POETRY COURSE

Assignment I
I enter the wood shed, a robin is there
vain-seeking the air, despairing and bare.
I weep, for he'd flee if he could.
I cry, for I'd fly if *I* could.
  AVOID THE BANAL, HACKNEYED, TRITE, TRIVIAL
  SHALLOW AND UNINTERESTING. STRIVE FOR DEPTH.

Assignment II
Oh, intricate Jeremiad,
wistful Pythagorian theora...
plumbing your Faustian phenomena
I philisticate, mystically.
  MAKE POETRY NOT ENCYCLOPEDIAS. AVOID
  THE PSEUDO-INTELLECTUAL. STRIVE FOR WARMTH.

Assignment III
Impassioned lover, fired by a million suns,
whose molten tongue dissolves my timid ear,
at whose least breath my trusting eyelids melt,
why must you lava ashes on my heart?
  COOL DOWN! UNDERSTATE. IMPLY. TANTALIZE.
  SUGGEST. LEAVE ROOM.

Assignment IV
Gloom. Deep, deep
mere echoes of   Echoes of what, of why,
    and more compelling, where....
  Is it this glistening
thinned despair?
  COME BACK TO EARTH. MAKE SENSE.
  OBSCURITY NOT THE NAME OF THE GAME.

So.
Obscurity is not the name of the game.
Well, I have news for *you*, Sir!

You're the one who's obscure.
You're the one who doesn't make sense.
I don't know what the hell you're talking about
half the time.
   BIG IMPROVEMENT. LAST ASSIGNMENT SHOWS
        FIRMNESS,
  COMMAND, CONTROL. SEND MORE OF SAME.

                Frances M. Greene

THE TIMID AUTHOR'S LAMENT

It is difficult
when you were raised in Snapdragon, Tennessee,
by two people who never missed a PTA meeting
and who were so proud the day your first poem
appeared in *Jack and Jill*;
and when you have an aunt who has taught sixth grade
practically since she was in sixth grade
and neighbors who sit fanning their front porches
and discussing the latest Communist threat...

it is difficult, I say,
under these circumstances to let go and write
freely about this man and woman who got together
in a deserted railroad station and, uh

                Frances M. Greene

SNAKE HANDLER AT THE FAIR

"Watch carefully," she said.
"I'm new with rattlesnakes."
Not a fool among us believed that.
She could have been of the cult
but for the way her delicate fingers
slipped through the cool diamond coils
and stroked him straight until
he yawned milk white venom
into a sterile, empty jar.
We burned from the easy way
she took his poison.

        J. Maurice Thomas

SONATA IN BROWN, FOR WOODWINDS

Brown is a philosophic dwarf,
the spirit of a once green wood
who sits invisible upon the highest bough
in the dry season
and counts his treasures like a squirrel his nuts.

Look down. It is a brown
November world. The gnarled, honed tree arms
burn brightly through their sleeves of varnished ice
and cast a gold illusion
upon the frost-pale, unexpectant sky.
The stoic, umber hills
glow warmly in the noncommittal east....
(Where does brown end and gold begin?)

Hush. It is the hoary hermit priest—
bone-stripped and weather-logged—
wanders the wooden way to his brown hut
for a last supper of acorns and dried roots.
He tells his patient beads
to a greek chorus of owls.
His words are borne away on burnished wings.

Behold, nine druids march from one brown cave.
(Earth-colored capes float on the dream-tossed air.)
They weave and circle round an ancient thorn,
chanting brown runes to the philosophic dwarf
(too high away to hear).

Listen. Down the vale. The droning woodsmen
are coming for the oldest, sagest trees.
What marvelous manuscripts they'll make!
What hand-carved treasure chests to store them in!
What portly chairs, what noble desks, what statues
of martyred saints.... What fragrant firewood
to grace a brown study.

In every shivering elm
the small brown animals huddle together
and stow away their griefs
for a long winter's sleep.

In her brown oak-bole home
a solitary, aging wood-nymph
rocks on her haunches,
hugging frozen knees
against her starved and swollen belly—
moaning for the horned and bleeding Spring.

      Esther Erford

FLUTE SONG

Love gone,
do you remember
the clarion call
to hunter's earth—
in the heady frost,
the hard blue burning?

Undone,
would I resemble
 (ever again)
the lark who sang
in the cloven nest
at the valley's edge,
by watercress streams,
in the rose-hipped morning?

I conjure you
down the lean years—
you who escaped
from the spinning town
to the stone cliffs
with your white-robed band—

to murder and create,
this side of yearning.

>   Esther Erford

>   it was raining then

when
spotted leaves
began their

trapeze paths
to earth. they fell
on thin-veined

wings,
fragile
like the clustered eggs
of fish.

they were
the ticker tape
of trees;
falling
on

the made-up clowns
below.

>   Jim Barry

ILLUMINATION

GRANDMA—
You lit your
candles every
night, and
the darkness
crawled over
the cliffs of your faith
while the smoke
smothered the fear
of your dying.
The pain remained
I suppose until—
Still
I can't help
hoping that
they have candles
where you have gone.
The color isn't important.

                Ruth Wildes Schuler

STERNAL

Dwarf stars hang
above satin moon,
while fish swim
through fragments of time.
Silver crystals crash
above Russian sabres,
while philosophers and poets
argue about the meaning
of ancient rites
and the location
of nebulas and black holes.

Myths are woven
through a tapestry of dreams,
and I break bread
against tomorrow's hope,
riding the back
of an angry wind.

      Ruth Wildes Schuler

"AYE, GOOD SAILOR, AYE"
(song for Cristi)

"I came to him as Sailor
From peaceful, imagined seas."
I left her fast as ever
For that land beyond the lees.

My girl she is a beauty, Aye
Thus sees old Sailor's eyes;
She gave me more than title, Aye
And she is more than bride.

Fairer soul than launched the crafts,
She's shown me that and more, Aye.
She guides me as I leave you,
Her place on yonder shore by.

      Danny M. Bounds

RETURN

It must
start
somewhere

In an iceberg's
molten speech

Or a frantic
babycry
of separation

An event
ignites

All the dreamwalks
of the
day's best

Sleepers
Awake to everything
Asleep to all

Returning:
the bond of

escapable reality
Pausing in
time's

rugged gaps

                        martin burwell

FIELDS

Fields have been
in my life more than
mountains
    or streams.

Running through
    plowing under
laying on.

I have no fear of returning
to fields.

                  Terry W. Brown

SHAME

I feel the bones
on my bare feet,
as I cross the burial ground
that now has my fence around it.

Every year when I plow
I find a few more arrowheads
and a new wave of shame.

                  Terry W. Brown

THE BEAST

The infant dropped from his mother's womb
    into the Beast's den.
Even then, among summer memories of boyhood,
    the hunter was with him,
Pursuing child's laughter down back streets
    and alleys of Sandusky.
The lion waited;
Its soft footsteps silently
Pacing through his dreams.

Church stand firm, unmoving as a mountain.
Stone cross at the summit
Portraying Christ's agony, Man's agony.
Weary pilgrims struggle up the ascent
Over pitfalls, over chasms,
Seeking to scale the heights,
Praying for a place of rest.
In a rock grotto is a golden statue
    of the Virgin,
Our Lady of Immaculate Conception.
Across this sterile landscape
    roams the lion:
They came together, woman and man,
Frightened creatures fleeing the hunter;
Each seeking strength neither had to give.
No longer children, still
They awkwardly touched,
His searching hands roamed over her:
But savage apathy killed all emotion
As love lay dead before the Beast.

The carnival land
Fades to darkness;
Summer people wearing circus smiles disappear.
Night advances,
Formless shadows merge into lurking fears
On the silenced gaity of artificial laughter.
The hunter emerges from darkness rising to the sky

As if to devour stars and heaven,
As if to pounce on the man's shuddering face.
Ravagings of the Beast are terrible, mighty;
Before its power we are like struggling prey
Held fast in the lion's jaws.

                John Roth

PRAYER OF A PRODIGAL SON

Our Father, art thou in heaven?
Hollow is thy name.
Will thy kingdom come,
Is thy will done on earth,
Is it done in heaven?
Begrudge us this day
Our weary bread.
And forgive not our trespasses
As we forgive those who trespass
    against us.
Why are we lead into temptation
And delivered unto evil:
All men?

                John Roth

VOICELESS

I could cry out loud
And no stars would answer,
My joy or anguish swallowed by space
Or absorbed by some nebula.
I could speak but what would it matter—
Earth makes no recognition,
Its reply mockery—
Echoes or the sound of life.

I am removed from this place and time
By my heart and vision;
Their sharpness which cleaves
The thinnest mist or dourest stone
Shatters my armor as well
But I am a mist with volition;
I cannot be held by any hand
Nor blown by any wind.

I am a presence older than stars;
I am a black hole where nothing escapes
But my passion and rage
Fed by all I consume,
A vampire in a bottomless grave
Where all will come with and without time.

I could cry out but I refrain
And incandescent spheres are unmoved,
Stars still wheel in their courses.

                                      Dwight E. Humphries

THREE PARTS A LONELINESS

I.

Here we are
Gathered together
Beginning to starve,
Forgetting to put out
The blistering fire,
Letting the room smoke up
Disaster.

II.

The fireman came
At three A.M.
Smouldering, cracking
The windows, the street
Ablaze with light.
Where's my splintered
Bones? At home?

III.

Carry me off to
Another country
Where the air is
Cleaner. Carry me to
A place that I haven't
Been to before. Let these
Ghosts appear.

                        David Vajda

DESCENT

Spiraling down the stairs
You pause to catch my eye

You impale me on the landing
Transfixed beneath you

Music from below can't rise
I stand within my shadow

Your legs silken my spine
Your perfume startles me

You pass without a turn
Without a sigh to affirm

Now your fuse in baser music
While I pulse here in stone.

William M. White

TO AN ONLY SON NEWLY DEPARTED FOR COLLEGE

How does it feel to hang up your coat
To make a bed and keep track of things
You rise straight and tall and smiling
A trifle cocky and vaguely lost

It's me that's empty
Missing the music of your room
The quickness of your prance
And the restless daze you dwell in

When I recline in the lounger
To watch the Sunday games
Yours is a ghost beside me

Well I have my harem you know
Your mother and your sisters
Still— still
I recall the way you walk or stand
Too much with it to bear it
Yet slightly apart from it all.

                    William M. White

THE HERMIT THRUSH

A small brown bird is singing,
is singing a fire in a clearing:
A circle of light and warmth
      you step into suddenly.
The thrush is a shape of flame and so
      are you,
and you are a shadow.
The thrush is a shadow of a shadow.
The thrush is a small brown bird,
      is singing,

                    Robert Dunn

THREE DAY WEEKEND

Our morning was blessed—
we blessed each other
and walked in snow.
Now the house is quiet,
those odd, swift hours
of early afternoon
quickly clamped
into a winter evening.
Everything turns,
shadows gnaw
the snowy slope
outside the window.

I am afraid to leave
the house, afraid
that darkness will appear
while I'm gone,
and that I will return
to find my third day
fallen from the calendar.

At last the snow is pale blue;
it gleams through the window
like a ghost land,
weeds and grass
inked on its surface.
Still the maple sapling
has not dropped its leaves.
They cling like
clotted bandages.

       Chris Ager

MASON, TURK AND MARKET

Two drunks
Curse each other
In Greek as the J car
Bangs past the corner,
Its antenna leaking sparks.

A face in the window
Mirrors that of the woman
Standing beside the curb:
Round, Oriental,
Her lips tight against her teeth.

The drunks stop,
Squint. One of them
Gropes for the other's sleeve,
His blunt fingers turning
As though lifting and sizing a grape.

The other nods.
Their shoulders bump
As they stumble into the gutter,
Silently. The woman rubs
Her pitted, painted cheek.

       Robert Joe Stout

COME, AND SPREAD THE SIGHT!

Outward flares the pattern's eye—
    when the dawn unfurls
a Monarch's gold to the retina
as curve and flutterings,
or it could be a robin's chevron,
mushroom up a treetrunk laddering,
magnolia in white profusion,
stone's blue sound in waters thrown,
or the consummate spray of sparrows;
things so thickly dreamt are owned,
homage brightens the marrow.

At that point,
the merest walk is multiplied—
shades of green in wind
that the sun unwinds in forms, a clean
communion you will smile for
no clear reason others see,
breaking to another's eyes
in secret flashes kindling
more patterns here,
shoot to the health of hearts
pierced gently, light to petals' opening.

                        Salvatore Salerno, Jr.

MOTHER

Mother — darken my
Store of troopsing

Memories in tinny
Toyland the way
You used to —
Rubbing, rubbing now
The light hardens
Me away from You

And back again
Pivot armed they
Swing, swing and
Bring back marches—
And I can only see
Me and the hand

That bends behind
Bins of grenadiers
Whose tin heads
Find me creosoting
Wooden virgins
To their beds.

Wail Mother —
Filled with haste
I raced today
To masturbate the
World away. (Forgive
My sinful way).

Tomorrow brings
Another day.

     Randy Weinstein

SMALL DESOLATIONS

it's strange
after all these years
I still half-remember
a walled strip of school gravel
the bleached portico of a Romanesque building
a wooden desk
steaming radiators
and the musty odor of damp coats

when I was nine years old
Mrs. Grant
my third grade teacher
showed the class
color slides of her trip to Italy
in Pompeii there was a small dog
wide-eyed with terror
still chained to its post

I am bound
by such threads from the past
which are woven into
the pattern of my days

                              Mike Lowery

MANY DEATHS

there
have been
  many deaths
since the both of us.
    many
    deaths and blood—
      since the both of us.

time has
ceased to caress us
    and
we
are left barren.
    barren.

there
have been
    many deaths
since the both of us.
    many
    deaths and blood —
      and we are left barren.

              Melissa Szymanski

LONG LIVE THE HILLS, THE HILLS ARE GONE

When the Masai were removed from their country to another in Kenya, a reservation, they transferred all the names for their hills and plains and rivers to the new land.

I stroll by calm, unruffled waters,
Still known to us as Babbling Brook.
The name contents me past all telling
(Although it bars too close a look).

And here I run through Happy Valley,
Where veldt and sward are withering.
Felicitous, you 'Happy Valley'!
Your memory is everything.

Then off to prowl the Woods Primeval:
Watch banded birds in well-trimmed park,
Where hewn Broad Arrow signs replace
'Umgai Loves Boolu' on the bark.

Whose woods these are I think I know,
Though words float so before my eyes
I think that I shall never see the trees
That nomenclature so transmogrifies.

By keeping names, our tribe preserves
Beliefs, both plain and mystic:
So much of our, and every, world
Turns out to be linguistic.

                        Philip Hughes

JADED GREEN

Through sunlit tresses of jaded green
Gentle flowing breezes
Symphonize
To the rituals of the great evergreens,
Swaying back and forth,
Back and forth,
Waltzing in the sun

Paying no heed to a dark and dreary
World at their feet,
They crowd together
To whisper of long forgotten secrets,
Ancient times,
Ancient things

The grove is deep,
Silent now with a rusted age,
Dark emerald shadows play fitfully
Among massive boughs,
Then a cry,
A moan, a sigh,
Breaks the sleep
Of a forest murmuring still

June W. Thornton

AT THE BREAK OF DAY

Above, the celestial canopy intensifies
Into a dense azure haze
As morning stillness sheaths
The budding day

Sun glints brightly
On dewy needles
As wisps of rising steam,
Curl,
Above the slowly warming ground
The air wavers and blurs
As the heat of day
Takes new strength
After night's numbing weariness

Green moss clings tightly
To cloak aging bark
Against probing wintry fingers
Of icy coldness

As forest giants shiver,
Shedding leaves drift down
Brilliantly painted landscapes
To blanket the plunging earth

Coldly sparkling rivelets
Jostle among massive boulders
Before joining to skip and hop
Down steeply wooded ravines

Now rare insects drone
In lazy spirals toward the sun
As the morning bloom ripens
Into another fruitful day

June W. Thornton

BROKEN COMMANDMENTS

The Lotus
over his grave
closes—opens
with each dead
    breath.

In a mine field
he wandered— looking
for the Lotus
each breath of the leaf
would detonate his world.

The Lotus
under his gravestone
turns purple from
dark explosions of each
    breath.

He asks Lawrence
if he knows the Lotus
could explode the whole world
so he couldn't stand next
to himself and breathe
another deep
    breath.

                      Kathleen Gillette

DRAWN-OUT GLUE
(from a painting by Jendrich Heisler)

Over the night-eyed town
he hovers, then sits
on the tip of a peaked roof.
He stretches
his great white wings
for balance
and begins to eat
the neighbor's house.

All down the street
the fish stand on their tails
alarmed at the sound
of chewing.

They look
out of their black windows
and see nothing
but snow sleeping
under the cold moon.

                      Judith Lindenau

The bridge,
   silently awaiting to flee,
moves through the night
   without steps...
      like a dream,
hidden away
   inside of me.

                David L. Meth

A LIFE

It has the usual appurtenances.
Raisable eyebrows. Bendable fingers
with little hard shells at the ends.

A mouth that snaps open and shut.
Movable eyeballs. An inverted navel.
It can pick up marbles with its toes.

It can feed itself,
drive an Oldsmobile,
set a delectable table,

sing *do re mi fa so la ti do.*
It has two of some things,
one of others. Everything fits,

like pipes. It breathes in oxygen,
breathes out carbon dioxide,
exactly as described in Biology One.

And yet, it is disappointed

                Phyllis Janowitz

THE TATTERED TOWEL

Our fortunes are small but overwhelming,
The presence of the stars between the shelves,
Between the nailed together shelves.
The sleeping dog, the tattered towel.
This is a coat of many colors,
A creation over the heart of painted flowers.

Painted flowers climbing, as roses, even beyond the sleeve.
If one half of this coat is half of each, then we
Are sewn together, the sewn together selves.
Each of us is engaged in a closed and sleepy flower,
Drinking together the dream inducing feathered colors;
All this gives light to the used weathered bowl.

      Nickie Gunstrom

NX211*

Out of an agrarian age he soared
Sprung from the rich soil of rugged individualism
A north star brilliancing across the consciousness of man
And the backdrop of his vanishing personal world,
The shadow of his chevron trailing and tearing the skies
 with the talons of everywhere iron birds
Cenotaphic contrails across the eyes of his era
Pained for the hopeful preservation of his beloved wild
 things,
And thsoe who lived and loved with this lincolnesque man
Saw in that invisible mountain of his cabanic courage
That high and distant aerie where he has gone to dwell
 with the gods.

      F. Anthony Blankenship

*Charles Augustus Lindberg
NX211 *The Spirit of St. Louis.*

ANNIE TACKETT

Annie Tackett
   was afraid of witches.
She knew people who were witches.
  she was afraid of them
    and took precautions —
she scared Jenny's mother
  when she was a child.
Annie Tackett
  was a witch herself;
   she was afraid
   of the Frenzy
  that welled up inside her
that knew & made pact with
  the slow disaster in the woods —

the Bacchae! the Bacchae!

  I walked up the hill
past the demon white chickens
  into the graveyard of
    Jenny's mother's family,
between the tall white-painted
    treetrunks,
& knelt by Annie Tackett's grave:

  "What do you see, Annie?"

"I see War, and Hate, and Horror,
   and a horrible Love!"

                Charles Upton

TO A YOUNG POET

Ripe hair.
What shouting ripe orange hair.
Roasted, it seems;
no, baked on a decade of sun.
A copper-polished bowl
or flaming silk;
wet rust.
Yellow and green flash
at roots;
young, restless fire.
Tones,
What brilliant themes
bounce off that head.

THOUGHTS AT A CONCERT

What kills spirits
  is doubt
    unsteady trust
      frail thoughts
        fear
Catacombs are easy
  each mind
  to its own cell
  remains unspoken,
    hung on barren walls
We are not victims
    yet
No rust on our bones
    nor limp roving blood
Not stone through lungs
    but music
  keeps our souls
    like hawks
above the broken earth.

                    Karolyn Pettingell

Ruby is going to marry a magician
He is Peter and tall
He wears suspenders and eats
You can see him at the restaurants
There are only two
Their last name will be White

On a cattle-car
coming to the edge of town and autumn
Ed is harvesting applause
He is inside a basket
He handles
He has handles

Good-morning gentle willow from the waltz-lands
Your movements know the raindrops names

                    Rick Ulman

CONVERSING: 12

"You must admit the love is dead;
but, knowing that, we are trying to
make the dying last a long time."

"What, look at the pleasant time we
had at the park Saturday. You act
as if our emotions have been murdered."

"Yes, exactly so. Smiles and rides on
a swingset make little difference.
The bullet is already implanted in the heart,
but the body takes awhile in crumpling.
We're just trying to keep the love
off the floor."

                    Kim Williamson

NEAR THE SUBWAYS

Every morning at 8
the newspaper stand
opens like a mouth.

Magazines porn its throat.
Small white racks are
rotting. Could all the
candy they hold be doing it?

An old man sells the
papers. Cold winds rub
his face red. When they
stop, Jack Daniels keeps
it that way.

Nearby subways belch
up customers. They nag
like a bad back over the
news that just went up
20 cents. A mayor ago
it was a dime.

					Kevin Pilkington

PRAYER

See me where I stand
that I may be tall.
Know me in my heart
that I may be kind.
Linger in my mind
that I may be wise.

					Bob Kaplan

INTRODUCTORY BOTANY

To make this book more
teachable and readable, we have left
out the chapter on thallophytes.
These plants are primitive,
so simple, like some people,
you will hardly miss them.

                        Ron McFarland

NEXT TUESDAY

If the UFO's are up there,
I'm waiting for them to turn
Denver, the mile high scar,
Into a quivering pile of protoplasm.
I'm waiting to see
The cars and people,
Trapped in the mounds of jello
Like ants in amber.
What are They?
With their universal sense
O' humor and power.

                        Carl Scott Harker

DECEMBER

sits in the mouth
like a refrigerator or
a set of iron teeth.
We have sold everything we owned
so that our hair can enter a condominium
in sun-lamped Miami Beach.
Meanwhile
in Philadelphia
we cannot remember where we put our dead
while one by one watches
and rings drop from us through the grate
of the heat register
where
our children's bogeymen ghosts
japanese movie monsters dracula the lighthouse
lady on Front St. tigers and sad clowns
wait to receive them
in a perpetual carnival of spring.

                              Norman Lock

NO. 260

damp autumn airs billowed
the back of his gray
flannel shirt as he
leaned sideward against
a brown brick station wall
near the public house rains fell
slowly
and in small streams stifling the
pavements dusty stench
and very green vines grew as
machines of various
ocher tones moved
evenly across
rain washed streets
beige silk lingerie
aired before an
open window
and red dogs
slunk around the corner.

                               Rennis H. Sees

SPRINGTIME IN DAVID WANN

To see me
slicing through
the city wind—
collar up, beard stubble,
hair wild,
dazed and bleary
from the graveyard
shift,
dawn about the hue
of a gray crayola,
car doesn't want
to start—

who would ever
guess that
I'm right on the verge
of bursting
into flower?

                  David Wann

ENIGMA

You jog past, legs smoothly churning
Through the early morning cold.

When not in motion,
Your body resembles a tall slab
Of New England granite.

Warm eyes betray your impassive face,
Shut like a clam against me.

                  Janet Ruth Heller

LITTLE QUICKIE

Snappy Comeback
Well, look who's here!

Left Dangling
I thought you were a goner this time
for sure.

Complete Surmise
Now I suppose you want to jump right
back in bed.

Right On Baby!
Just like that, huh?

Humbler Try
I was hoping you would say that.

Tempered Tantrum
Well, don't hold your breath.

Another Thing Coming
In fact, he should have been here an
hour ago.

Little Quickie
Gee, you don't lose any time, do you?

Robert J. Svoboda

THE KNOT

She was both there,
a dream unraveling
from a spool, the
multiplicity of language.

Many times started,
but never finished,
a riddle sitting on
its voice.

There a silence,
a return from sleep,
an underground stream
like the memory of sound.

His voice, not frightening
yet not in her language.
A set of legitimate demands,
weights on the wound.

The string all tangled
just outside her belly.
Had it been just tied
or untied?
Where did the dream begin
or her birth end?

                              Ian Krieger

ASKING TOO MUCH THIS TIME

While the body lies awake at night, each bone
pries itself loose — feels its way out along the hips,
   scampering off into directions.
The small fragments like white paint run out along
   country roads.
A floating rib on the right side takes a cab to the trains.
An upper vertabra wanders through deserted bus stations.
The fingers rattle in the phoneboxes of distant towns.
They fill the air.

With the first triangular ringing of a bird's beak
they return, crawling up the white bark of the moontree,
scrabbling with frightened noises at the window,
kicking unconnected against the drainpipe;
and as the alarm goes off there is no one to rise
   and let them in.

                              Jared Smith

UNDERWATER

rice birds chirping
rising sun
plumeria blossoms bursting

peeling off my clothes
I wade into
Kapaa Lagoon

warm green water glistening sun

underwater
blowing bubbles

I emerge
a silver bubble
bursting on
the surface

                    Thomas Hickenbottom

COMMUNION WITH THE DEAD

In the fluid,
paralyzing cold of
summer's death,
wading deep in the skeletal
symphonies of those of
an earlier time,
I came to know their helplessness
and the timelessness of age.

Transitory glimpses such
as those that sever
one from life are but
illustrations of
how all that is life
is not living.

Robert L. Wilson

ADDENDUM

The addendum of my life,
Which is I now living,
Is a short thing I made —
  Made miniature
To fit in agony
  The delicate patterns I prescribed,
And like a child kept in a box,
  I have lived subtly
In the duration of dying.

Jesse McKnight

WHAT TO DO

when the eyes that burn up your world
turn to ice: learn to wear wool;

when the dead deal out your life:
live twice;

when love unravels in your hands:
learn to sew with air,
your body like a needle to the sky.

Roger Weaver

SPRING OUTING

Today we step into a fine new season
air snaps
rain fine as needles
white sun glares behind the grey veil of morning
raindrops tap on the roof of the cabin
the farm brook roars
and the road slicked down for a date
takes our frozen winter secrets
over the bridge to town
where they are served on a hot platter.

Gudrun Mouw

MORNING MINE

Weeds, silver-frosted lithographs
   in the autumn cold fields
   draped here and there
   with tattered tapestries
   of Arachnae, abandoned
      long ago.

A crow, fingerpainted smudge
   on a child's blue sky,
   pulling clouds across the summer-worn
   golden sun, splashing shadows
      on the ground.

A farmhouse, grey wrinkled face
   with window-shade eyes shut,
   smoking pine-smelling wood,
   grumpily awakens to the sound of
      geese gossiping.

                Liz Wrenn

When I play tennis I don't think about it
I revel in the easy rush of air
Advance the score and shout it out
Swing my once-more
Supple muscles in the re-discovered
Glory of myself as graceful savage
Only when the racket head is covered
The balls canned up the rage
Of glad aggression calmed can
I realize what I am

                Gary Sterling

PEACE

"Be still
  and know
    that I
      am God."

Relax
  and think
    of Him.

And peace
  will fill
    your soul.

          Mary-Ruth Mundy

DIVINE POWER

  God
has power
to change the
vilest heart,
and redeem
it to full purity.

  Christ
is the hope
of the world;
  Remember
Him in this
greed world's
darkest hour.

          Mary-Ruth Mundy

SPIRITS

Who calls me? Who?
in darkened night
whose ghost wants me
and comes in sight?

A dear kind friend
who died too young
comes back to say
"Please see me mom."

This spirit's real
to me at night.
He does not stir
me in a fright.

My dad comes, too,
to chat with me
and comforts all
the family.

"This all seems strange,"
I hear you gasp.
You think it's queer,
you're scared to ask.

I don't query
my God Whose love
is all around,
below, above.
For in His Way
I strive to be,
and I am sure
He dwells in me.

                    Mary-Ruth Mundy

WITHOUT FEAR

I don't fear seeing ghosts
or dreaming that I hear
words of love from my friends
who've died and live again.

I can walk in darkness
among earthly dangers,
for what have I to fear
with Love inside my heart?

                        Mary-Ruth Mundy

FOR THE END TIMES

Be praised, my God,
in all I do
that I may serve
and glorify
Your creation.

Redeem mankind
that we may live
in harmony,
all worshipping
the one true God.

                        Mary-Ruth Mundy

EARTH'S REBIRTH

Golden barley, wheat and oats
glisten in the harvest time.
If I but toil down till dusk
all that I can reap is mine.

But before You made them mine,
Lord, You sent both rain and shine
and You caused each seed to grow,
touched them with Your Hand Divine.

Touch us with Your Hand Divine
that Your love will spread on earth.
Guide us forward, help us shine.
May all mankind live rebirth.

                    Mary-Ruth Mundy

MOTHER

She an old, old woman,
all alone, all alone,
no one to speak with her.
She's by herself at home.

Her legs are sore and so
she stays indoors and dreams
memories of husband's
and children's happy themes.

Why does she wait each day?
What is she waiting for?
A call from heaven home
that God's love has in store.

                    Mary-Ruth Mundy

FAITH

Today I saw a robin fly
against a clouded sky,
directly through the gathering storm
wending his sure way home.

Lord, make my faith like that small bird,
bravely, unerring, soaring,
making my way straight heavenward
to my God in glory.

Amen

>Mary-Ruth Mundy

HEATHER

Safe in my arms
my small Heather,
your little heart
is beating so
fast it flutters.

You are my heart,
my very soul,
promised rainbow,
My small daughter,
I love you so.

>Mary-Ruth Mundy

IN LENT

Early morning's
dew on the grass,
I move, silent,
and soon I pass
the corner and
go to Church Mass
praising my God
in quiet peace.

                                    Mary-Ruth Mundy

DIVINE DESTINY

The slender moon is descending in the west
and I glimpse Orion through tall dark pines.
Stately Pleides moves like a fine thin thread
across the heavens with jewel-like brilliance.

The planets reflect a distant greeting, too,
as they light my path along my lone life's way;
What intricate future do they plan for me
as they guide me to heavenly destiny?

                                    Mary-Ruth Mundy

A CHRISTMAS HYMN

At Christmas time
the angels sing
of Christ's glory
and man redeemed
by one Divine
Holy Savior.

If they should sing
then why don't I?
For Christ came down
to earth for me
whom He has loved
and saved by grace.

Dear God, my Lord,
may every heart
turn unto You,
receive Your grace,
accept Your love,
and sing Your praise.

Amen, Amen.

                    Mary-Ruth Mundy

A MIRACLE

I am very far from being perfect
but yet in God's mercy, He redeems me
and gives hope when all is bleak.
This, the miracle of my destiny.

                    Mary-Ruth Mundy

A GUIDANCE COUNSELLOR'S EVENING PRAYER

Dear Holy Father,
Thank you devoutly
for this day ending;
for goodness You gave,
loyalty of friends;
for echoes of truth
that dawned upon me
while guiding others
along life's hard path;
for your forgiveness
when I disappoint
young and trusting ones
who believe in me.
I ask that you, Lord,
give me courage and strength
and Your wisdom
to do what pleases
You and is right in
Your most Holy sight.
Guard me from dangers
and indecision,
from false pride and the discouragement
that can come easily.
Teach me to love you
in all that I do
and to give others
a glimpse of You in me
and in my thoughts.
May I care enough
to do my full best
with You as my Guide.
To You, dear God, I
pray for help. Amen.

                              Mary-Ruth Mundy

DAWN

In the solitude of morning
And lightness makes objects appear,
The stillness stimulates my mind,
No hurried din to interfere.

The friendly cat snuggles by me,
My children are still fast asleep,
I turn my thoughts to higher things,
Books to write and promises to keep.

Many daily tasks before me,
I sit in calm, thoughtful pose,
This seems to me some of heaven,
Perhaps it is, who really knows?

      Mary-Ruth Mundy

AUTUMN

In autumn, when we rake the leaves,
jump on piles growing higher,
we laugh and work and sing and play
then roast marshmallows by a fire.

We thank you, God, for all good things
around us to take delight in.
Keep us with You and with nature.
Your love surround us and within.

      Mary-Ruth Mundy

THE PLIGHT OF YOUTH

For turbulent homes and unhappy hearts
we breath a prayer, God, for Your holy peace.
Bring love and help and Your calm tenderness
and may bickering cease.

This is the prayer of many teenagers,
confused, disappointed, groping for sense
in a place where misery adds to grief.
Lord, remind them of Your Omnipotence.

                        Mary-Ruth Mundy

IN PURSUIT OF EXCELLENCE

The quality of excellence is strained;
Today it is almost non-existant.
You need a plumber — any service man —
and you hold your breath and pray fervently
that he knows what he should be doing and
he won't charge more than a month's groceries
then leave without fixing what needed it.

Where is man's pride in performing his best?
Is this feeling lost between his skill
and the daily work he does for others?
Does he no longer see that the goal of
perfection brings him close to our Maker?
Is excellence no longer important?

                        Mary-Ruth Mundy

A PRAYER FOR ALL MANKIND

A cry for unity
in the dark wilderness,
scandal of history,
fear and anxiety,
distrust, superstition
and fierce nationalism.

In Ecumenism
may all come together
in the Spirit of one
body of our Savior
whose Holy name we bear;
come universal Love.

Mary-Ruth Mundy

AFTER THE STORM

Now the roaring winds have stilled
and the calm silence hurts our ears.
We strain our limbs and try to move
our bodies numbed by chilly fears.

No new flowers lift their blossoms,
blades of grass thrust up densely green.
A little child lifts face and hands
to a bird singing songs serene.

Mary-Ruth Mundy

THE TOAD

Toad sits in a corner
just guzzling down his beer,
croaking out the orders
all rudely loud and clear.

His wife toiled all day
to earn the board and bread.
When she came home again
she cooked and made the bed.

"I liberate my wife!"
says he, with one big grin,
"for she earns the money
and I spend mine on gin."

                     Mary-Ruth Mundy

TO SEVEN CANADA GEESE

Canada geese, tell me, please,
do you honk to haunt and tease,
telling me that winter's near
and you're flying south of here?

Canada geese, will you roam
over meadows and seas foam,
take me with you in your flight,
make my lonely heart delight?

                     Mary-Ruth Mundy

GEORGIA O'KEEFE PAINTS

Goergia O'Keefe paints a flower
                    like a world
a huge white world, a red,
a smooth cool fragrant world
with stamens thrusting upward.

She paints the world
                    like a flower
an orbiting blossom perfuming the wind,
respiring planes of color
and towers pounding skyward.

The globular depth in her poppies
    the gasp in her mountains
    the uncanny soul in her eyes:
large truths are small and smallest mightiest.
We cannot see unless we choose to look.

                        Marilyn Throne

Orpheus played silence in his song
To embrace the notes that lingered long
Over what he knew of love

And thought his song's embrace
Would silence his disdain
For love that showed haste.

He little knew love
Who sought again new song
That played around her face.

                        Jennifer Nostrand

AT THE SHORELINE

smoke-blue, winged
straw sticks for legs
mute in marsh waters
in flight the heron
flakes power through
consciousness in clean
thrusts of beauty
claiming a stake in
memory forever.

                         Harland Ristau

5/1

welcome to four o'clock;
after all, the brilliantly lit park:
two speckled balls, two
fat pigeons coast
chain rails on the wooden foot bridge which
on the lagoon slapping red motorboats,
flowered very young ladies
carrying pretty, cheap parasols,
their paper and colored Japanese inks so bright,
spring before your eyes.

                         John Thomas Stovall

THE SIGN IS DOWN

Aimlessly I drove my car.
I needed someone to talk to,
Even better, a good listener,
And as I drove near your home, my friend,
I knew you would.
I followed the well-worn path,
Seeking the familiar sign on your lawn,
There so many months.
Your home was before me,
But I knew I was too late.
Strange children play on your lawn
And the sign is down.

                                        Charles V. Olynyk

A STRONG DISSOLVE

Am I old? Am I fair?
Are there garlands in my hair?
If I sweep now, shall I sweep it all in place?

Am I weathered? Is there guile
In this mannered, makeshift smile?
If I reap now, has the reaping kept apace?

Soft! Be mute, my martinet.
Mask my marrow. No, not yet.
For I weep now, and the weeping will efface.

                                          Ronica Stern

GALLERY

A splash of paint had erupted
Into a work of art.
A bystander scratched his head
Yet couldn't play in the part he shared.
Some others felt they got the cue.

A dot like a moon filling oblivion
Affronted measurement of facing wall.
A bystander stood before it lost
As a guard called: "Closing time!"
After all, was that the plot?

                        E. Manuel Huber

MY LOVE'S EARS

My love's ears are sea
shells. Ocean swells of our bodies
sway the long kelp gently in their green
beds; long brown hair, her body the color
of sand, smooth as sanded driftwood. The tides

We are the tides moving the oceans
in and out of estuaries and bays
exposing each and then covering all others.
No moon today, bright sun, a school
of fish swim between us
and are trapped in the nettings of our bodies.

                        WDTimmerman

GLANCING IN ON A BRAND-NEW HIGH-RISE APARTMENT FOR ELDERLY PEOPLE

A bare linoleum lobby

A dozen woman and one man
All at least sixty
Sitting on folding chairs
Looking at sheet music
Facing a piano

Their lips are moving

We cannot hear what they are singing

                    Joe C. Ireland

SOME PEOPLE

Some people seldom see the moon
   Or feel the ecstasy
Of music, as it fills the room...
   Or mirrored sun on sea.
Some people see...without the mood
   Which sensitivity
Puts into beauty, when pursued.
   That isn't true with me!
I feel with every sense I have...
   Inherited or learned;
Each sensation, I grasp and save
   For pages yet unturned.

                    Glenna Glee

GENUFLECTIONS

may day processions needed so much
practicing to get it right and then
those nuns had a thing about touching
your knees each time you neared a pew
or maybe a statue that seemed holy but
one could not be sure so genuflections
reigned supreme and each kid tried his
best or hers to do it right while clicking
nuns scurried down the aisle to stop an acolyte
from burning his cassock by friday when we all
would meet outside with the bishop for one last
show-down and sing oh mary we crown thee with possums
today

Larry Rochelle

NOTICE

Carefully staged proclamations on my slick door
flutters of lists on iron walls
for I am a careful woman
Notices Names Sources Hours Maps Maxims
jockey me
hedge a wedge of desk
a coat tree stabbing a cape
a brimmed Baja catbird hat
Past present and future calendarized and clocked
hatted and cloaked
Careful

Nancy Stone

DRINK IT DOWN

If that cutie in the chorus
Wears a brevity that's porous
And her wink excites a gentleman in town;
Though your heart may pound and flutter,
Keep your mind out of the gutter,
Drink it down, drink it down, drink it down!

Drink it down Methusalah,
Drink it down, Grandad,
Though the girls may kiss your shiny pate,
Remember that it's late, too late,
Drink it down, drink it down, drink it down!

If a baby smiles "come hither,"
So your nerves are in a dither,
And you wonder what's behind her pretty crown,
Don't reply until you're certain
What's the game of her who's flirtin',
Drink it down, drink it down, drink it down!

Drink it down, Methusalah,
Drink it down, granddad,
Though the girls may kiss your shiny pate,
Remember that it's late, too late,
Drink it down, drink it down, drink it down!

If you're crazy for a lady,
And she intimates, yes, maybe,
If you'll buy a mink she wants of golden brown;
Watch the signs that show the reason
Why old suckers are in season,
Drink it down, drink it down, drink it down!

Drink it down, Methusalah,
Drink it down, granddad,
Though the girls may kiss your shiny pate,

Remember that it's late, too late,
Drink it down, drink it down, drink it down!

John Warwick Daniel III

THE PORNOGRAPHY OF GUILT

The brown eyebrows of the lonesome tailor
fuse as he fingers your garment, his hands
so creased with backroom use he hardly
recognizes them. Into your face he says
look at this it's all busted ya gotta have
a new one it's off the track
and so indicted you walk off into
a street full of bakeries
aware of your thighs rubbing
casually together

Streaming towards the stoplight
with its three rounded options
like a woman drowning in the
perversity of an extra breast
she is blamed for,
you dream of a white seamless world.

Binnie Klein

ONE YEAR LATER

I have no words with which to spell the night.
I walk into our room, your bed is made,
Your clothes all neatly hung (they always were)
The brass bell on the table left for you
To call me (which you never used)
You proud in all the ways a man can be
Whose bones were molded intricately fine
And now your bones are crumbling in your grave,
And I must salvage what I could not save.

How shall I bridge the days now you are gone,
Rereading letters, filing things away,
Shuffling the words that throb, the empty night,
And yet there are no tears, the voice is still,
The agony is dormant and I sleep
The troubled sleep of one enmeshed by guilt
Who heard you calling in the tortured night
And did not hear the bell you never rang.

                        Hannah Kahn

THE CAPTURED

She swore truth
& cuddled, snug
in her bondage.

He like the heated stallion
gave up his graze,
left the hills of sweet grass
for pace hardened ground.

Now in sleep she clings
tight to his depth of chest,
while he runs unfettered
till the bridle hour of morning.

                              Anthony C. Kallas

ON PARANOIA

Goldilocks,
you have counted them
over and over again—
all those mean tricks
Papa Bear, Mama Bear.
and any other bear
played on us (but mostly you)
in a rush of bad times.
Counting both chairs,
the hard bed, the soft bed,
soup too hot or cold,
and inconsiderate
interruptions along
with other indignities,
you have convinced me
the plot points (my face is red)
in the right direction.

                        Lois V. Walker

POEM THIEF

He went, taking all my poems with him.
At his side Poetry frisked and danced,
tossing back over her shoulder a saucy farewell:
"Go back to your laundry, sweeping, vacuuming;
what did you think — that it was *he* who loved?
He was willing to service you, that's all."
She winked at me. Her magical eyes sparkled,
those diamonds she'd thrown to me in a velvet bag,
urging, "Into your eyes with them: see how life can shine!"
When she yanked them out later, it was pulling teeth—
worse: she left me not just bleeding... but blinded.
"Too bad," she called now, laughing, still still laughing,
all passion and joy mocking me standing there cold.
"Good-by— you won't see *me* again!" —As for him,
he didn't even bother to look back.

                                Doris Wight

PEACHES OF HOGBACK HILL

Before the big fire
the black-branched peach trees
buzzed in summer
and you complained the hill was
too alive.
Then you were left to bloom like an orphan,
alone. Under the petals of your frilly hats
you settled into a plumpness,
becoming the one always asked
to bake deep-dish pies
for family picnics.
But even with ten children
to kiss that ripe fuzzy cheek you offered,
there was still something missing
on the hill.

                          Gail Festa

SHOTGUN

In veiling atmosphere of smoke they sit
(while distant cousins drink warm beer and laugh)
and contemplate the gold of wedding bands,
immersed in thoughts of loneliness and love.

The narrow space between them holds no words;
a citadel of silence they devise
to cope with struggling thoughts that threated smiles
the proper social acting-out of joy.

The silent space is strained, yet stays intact;
compassion needles each the other's hurt.
They turn, and through their meeting eyes, they know
that this must be some terrible mistake.

                                            Scott Thomas

YOUR MORE, MY LESS

i draw you on tight as a sock:
i button you up along my chest, even
button the collar tight: i pull
you up my legs, i zip you tight
tight tight, close close, never tight
or close enough: i cinch the belt
of you tight, your shoes pinch my heels,
i walk on you, breath through you,
stretch your flesh with my use and bag
and tear you with misuse; and never
can i use you, tear, wear, close with you
enough to satisfy my craving.
so i insure your failure. your more
or less is always less the more i rave for.

Lance Lee

WE CAME TO CLEAN
WE AIM TO

Two eyes canvass for the woman
pass over visible housewives
their kids their laundry
mostly of dirt grease stains
and odors invisible

A radio blares
a fat lady stares
while his eyes glean
some handle clean
laundry with affection
with distraction
to the man

Women now nervous
some eyes wide
above magazines or below them hide
his eyes find much pink gum
in many pink mouths
oral boredom
the same color as seas of cactus curlers

Washing machines hump clothes
whirlpooling them to exhaustion
DON'T SIT ON THE WASHERS
a sign does say
They do
guarding their clothes with their weight
rhythm humming through fat groins
pelvises shake in pleasure fed by coins

Her name? Her description?
She was here last Saturday
and the week before
he had sketched her face
her body
her body without clothes

She had made love to her lingerie
folding caressing
an act of spatial undressing
he was mesmerized by her apparel
in the dryer-permanent press cycle
whirling like a tumbleweek tornado

No
she is not here today
he would say
—Nothing is permanent
beyond the present
cycles end
marked by time clicks
we never do
forget them—

       Debrie Stevens

NESTING

Hawk beak, pheasant hair:
something obscene in the outline of your fine-boned leg
makes me ready to swallow even the distance in you.

As the crow flies, you are far enough.
Maybe this gravel and corn will combine to bloom:
some common flower, cold as your red pretty heart,
a flag we can unite under.

Spurred to call my name, your breath comes frantic,
hard wings beating in my ear.
I grab for fields of poppies,
your hair wild in my clawing fingers.

                              Ruth Laney

YES

Yes to your body lying close
Yes to your smile
your eyes that read mine

Yes to the way you hold me
pelvis to pelvis
tongue to tongue

Yes to your love
growing new seasons
on my face.

                              Manna Lowenfels-Perpelitt

HOLDING TANK

There are snakes in her stomach:
she can feel them coiling,
growing inside
like giant fists,
the cocks of men.
Soon the black
flood will begin,
spilling down
between her thighs
in solid swarms.
And she will be helpless
to hold back the birth,
watching her own
flesh disappear;
knowing that no
amount of blood
will ever be enough.

                              Eileen Stratidakis

AFTER WORK

I know you.
I've unbuttoned your shirt
Countless times
As you gazed out the window
And the bus driver
Calmly shifted gears.

> C. A. Smith

COUNTERPOINT

I've been playing this blues guitar
Far, far too long.

Strumming gaily
On things as they are,

Picking out tunes
Like a super-star

Changing short to long
And right to wrong

Treble to base
In the cleft of my song.

Somewhere in the truth of it
I lost my ear for the music:

The sound, squeezed from calloused fingers,
Plucked out wrong—

The notes were clear,
But not the song.

> Michael S. Glaser

PHOTOGRAPHER/CLOWN

It's the sad faces she maps
And frames.
Her portfolio grows
Like stunted trees,
A slug trail
Across weed-grown roads
And faceless windows,
The glass wrinkled
From so much weather.

It's easy to hide in the spotlight
Behind white masque, bulbous nose
And glittering lashes,
Shoes so long
They make the children laugh.

Hills roll like film
Between towns. She knows
How the land lies boxed in.
Between takes
It is dark inside.

In one photo she shows
She's there—
Protected from the inside out—
Reflected in one window
Looking out the other.

                        Susan Landgraf

ABOUT OUR CONTRIBUTORS

The following abbreviations are used in contributor entires: "et all" for and others; "J." for Journal; "mag(s)" for magazine(s); "Pr." for Press; "Q" for Quarterly; "Rev." for Review; "Univ." for University. Months are abbreviated and U.S. Postal initials are used for states where appropriate.

Chris Ager, a graduate of the Univ. of Washington in Seattle, lives in the borough of Queens, NY.

Joanne Amadeo is editor of *Vega** and has published in England, Sweden, and Brazil. She is the featured poet in the March 1978 issue of *Third Eye*. Her book of poems, *Inner Space, Outer Space,* was publsihed in 1977.

Nova Trimble Ashley has been Kansas Poet of the Year three times. She has published six books and has appeared in *McCall's, Ladies' Home J., Good Housekeeping, Kansas Q., The Humanist, The Forum,* et al.

Jim Barry writes: "Over-schooled and under-educated, I still survives. A Pisces, I live by the sea of tranquility, seeking its support. Good poetry is that which works and invades the individual's aura. I think minimal poetry does it best."

Guy R. Beining writes: I work in a blasted bank; am approaching 1500 poems accepted; and my fourth and fifth chapbooks due out by autumn are 'Ogden's Diary and Voice 2' (Zahir Pr.) and 'The Butcher Dreams' (Realities Pr.)."

Benjamin Scott Blake's poetry has been published in a variety of little mags and newspapers and in a pamphlet, "Ben Blake's Greatest Hits" (1972). "The poet's ambition is to make a living as a writer. He would also like to go to the Moon, and eventually to become a duck."

F. Anthony Blankenship has appeared in the *J. of Popular Culture, The Lake Superior Rev., Major Poets, Cyclo-Flame, American Atheist, Melody of the Muse,* and *Poetry Today.*

Lucile Bogue has taught in London, Versailles, Rome, Vienna, Managua, San Miguel de Allende, Guayaquil and Tokyo. Founder of a college in Colorado, she recently won the $1500 Grand Prize in the world of Poetry Contest in San Francisco. She is writing a book on Yeats.

Danny M. Bounds is in the U.S. Army working and studying in Italy.

Terry W. Brown "has published in 50 small magazines and newspapers, the most notable being *Grit, The Phoenix Gazette, The Seattle P-I,* the *Firelands Arts Review* and the *Kansas Q.*"

Martin Burwell, a classical musician, has appeared in *The Huron Rev., Wind, Green's Mag., The Lamb, Aim, Capper's Weekly, The Hartford Courant,* et al.

Marilyn Carmen is a Penn State senior. In three years she has had nearly 200 acceptances of her work and eight awards and five prizes for poetry and prose.

Melissa Clark, a dancer, has published in *Catalyst, The Smith, Poetry View, ASFA Poetry Q.,* the *Seneca Rev., Green's Mag., Buffalo Spree,* et al. HBJ Jove published her novel, *Devlyn,* in 1977.

John Warwick Daniel III has two collection of poetry, *O Coming Age* (Bruce Humphries, 1940) and *Zenith Quest,* soon to be published.

Robert Dunn has published *Poems For A Meeting Place* (1968), *A Cantata For Groundhog Day* (1971), *Counting Stars on Blue Mountain* (1972), *Green Leaf, Green Bough* (1975), all with Greenleaf Books, and *Apples and Thieves* (New Adams Pr., 1972).

Esther Erford has published in *Poet Lore, Lake Superior Rev., Western Poetry, Encore, Quoin,* et al.

Gail Festa has appeared in *Rolling Stone, Cosmopolitan, Best Friends, Images, Circus Maximus , Third Eye,* and *Whisky Island Q.*

Kathleen Gillette has appeared in *Carousel Q., Modus Operandi, Senior Edition, The Fringe Pr.,* and *The*

Rockfield Rev. Her first book of poetry was published in 1976.

Michael S. Glaser has published in *The Cottonwood Rev., Quartet, Poet Lore, The Lake Superior Rev., Circus Maximus, Poem,* et al.

Glenna Glee is a twice-widowed ex-GM employee. A Certified Master Graphoanalyst, she has published in *Poet, North American Mentor, Hoosier Challenger, Valley Views, American Poet,* et al.

Frances M. Greene lives in Muncy, PA.

Nickie Gunstrom has appeared in *South Dakota Rev., Decotah Territory, Calyx, 10 Point 5, Moving Out, North Stone Rev., Lamp in the Spine,* et al.

Carl Scott Harker writes: "In '76 I gave up cars for the Bicentennial, then pedaled to San Francisco on my bicycle. I am now living in heavy Oakland where I eat sunflower seeds and wonder what food looks like without artifical coloring."

Janet Ruth Heller helped to found the contemporary anthology *Primavera* in 1974. She has appeared in *Encore, The Spoon River Q., The Reconstructionist, Poetry of the Year,* and the *J. of Popular Culture.*

Thomas Hickenbottom has written three unpublished books of poems. He lives in the Santa Cruz Mountains.

David Holdt has appeared in *Maine Life, This Singing World, The Boston Univ. Spectrum, Chelsea, The Hartford Courant,* et al. *Sun Through Trees*, a poetry collection, was published in 1973.

E. Manuel Huber writes: "At a youthful age fell in love with 'Out of the Cradle Endlessly Rocking.' Schooled in Merchantville, NJ, and at Ursinus College, PA. Served in USMCWR in WW II. Last fifteen years have worked for the College of Physicians of Philadelphia."

Philip Hughes taught college for twelve years and left teaching to write full time.

Dwight E. Humphries has been editor of the *Georgia State Univ. Rev.* He is currently working on two chapbooks.

Joe C. Ireland has appeared in *Bitterroot, Cafe Solo, Dalliance, Dust, Poet Lore, The Smith, Sparrow* and *Born Into A Felony: An Anthology of Prison Writings.* He is author of *Short Order* (Forum Pr., 1974).

Phyllis Janowitz's book, *Rites of Strangers,* was chosen as 1977 winner of the Associated Writing Program contest and will be published by the Univ. Pr. of Virginia in the fall of 1978.

Anthony C. Kallas's chapbook, "Rock River Suite," was published by Sangamon Poets Pr. He has appeared in *Stone Country, Snakeroots, East River Anthology, Aspect,* et al.

Hannah Kahn is author of the book *Eve's Daughter* and has appeared in *Harper's, Poetry, American Scholar, Saturday Review, Yankee,* et al. She was poetry review editor for the *Miami Herald* for fifteen years.

Bob Kaplan is a radio-tv broadcast engineer turned freelance writer. His new book of poetry, *Voices In The Wind,* will be published Nov. 1978.

Binnie Klein has published in many mags and appeared in *Ardis Anthology of New American Poetry.*

Ian Krieger is associate editor of *Telepoem & Acceptances.* He is "working on a complete metaphysical guide to the iconology of Los Angeles."

Ventatesh Srinivas Kulkarni has appeared in *The DeKalb Literary Arts J., The Kansas Q., The Connecticut Fireside,* et al. He teaches and is director of the AIDP Humanities program at Grambling State Univ.

Susan Landgraf is a journalist/photographer in Washington State. She has published in many small mags and has conducted workshops in prisons and schools.

Ruth Laney has appeared in *Intro 5* and *Southern Writing in the Sixties, The Southern Rev.,* et al. Her work also appears regularly in *Runner's World* and *Track and Field News.*

Lance Lee has had plays produced in Los Angeles, Chicago, New Haven, and at the O'Neill Center's National Playwrights' Conference. He has appeared in *Poem, Lake Superior Rev., Midwest, Poetry Rev.*, et al.

Linda Lerner was born in Brooklyn, grew up there, and now teaches at Brooklyn College.

Judith Lindenau has appeared in *Noeva: Three Women Poets, A Change in Weather* (poetry anthology), the *Firelands Arts Rev., Offspring, Washout Rev.*, and *Poetry//Wheatfield.*

Norman Lock has "published poetry and fiction in many American rev.s and little mags. He is founding member of the Philadelphia New Language Action.

Manna Lowenfels-Perpelitt has appeared in *Gallimaufry, Women: A J. of Liberation, Red Weather, Passage II, Twigs, Connections, Poetry Now, Praxis*, et al. *Changing Masks,* a book of poems, will be published in 1978 by Buffalo Books.

Mike Lowery has appeared in *Encore, Nimrod, Image, Wind, Scree, Green's Mag., Coe Rev., Kansas Q.*, et al.

Ron McFarland is poetry editor of *Slackwater Rev.* and editor of *Snapdragon.* His chapbook, "Certain Women," was published in 1977 by Confluence Pr. A collection of twenty poems was recently published by *Audit Poetry.*

Jesse McKnight has appeared in *The Smith* and in *College On Your Own* (Bantam, 1977).

David L. Meth has appeared in *The American Pen, Neworld, Jeopardy, Lake Superior Rev., Hoosier Challenger, Valley Views, Poet Lore,* et al.

Frank D. Moore lives and teaches in Philadelphia.

Gudrun Mouw has been assistant poetry editor of *Anomaly* and has appeared in *Bitterroot, Three Sisters, Yoga J., Cape Rock J., Graffiti,* et al.

Mary-Ruth Mundy holds doctorates in both philosophy and psychology and is a guidance counsellor in Nova Scotia. She has appeared in *The Brandon Sun, The New*

Nation, The Forgotten People, and *The Manitoba Teacher.*

Jennifer Nostrand has published in *Kansas Q., Mississippi Rev., Modus Operandi, Spoon River Q., Indigo,* and *Connecticut Fireside.*

Charles V. Olynyk's background is in anthropology. He has written one novel and is working on a second.

Karolyn Pettingell is a puppeteer who has studied under Karl Shapiro and has published in *The California Q.*

Kevin Pilkington's "work has appeared in numerous publications in the United States and Europe." He is on the Writing Staff at the New School for Social Research in NYC.

Susan Irene Rea has been a participant in the Blue Ridge Writers' Project in Virginia and has appeared in the *Firelands Arts Rev.,* et al.

Harlan Ristau lives in Milwaukee, WI.

Larry Rochelle has published in *Aim Mag.* and *Hyacinths and Bisquits.* He writes: "I have a family of four kids, Nick, Doug, Dave, and Heather, who along with my wife, Ruth, live in a rented suburban house with our dog Misty who needs a shampoo badly."

John Roth has published in the *Firelands Arts Rev.* and the *Firelands Lamp.*

Salvatore Salerno, Jr., has appeared in *Ararat, Descant, Wormwood Rev.,* and *Graffiti.* He has published a collection of parables, *Dawn Over New Jerusalem* (Maya Pr., 1977).

Ruth Wildes Schuler was featured poet in the 1978 Spring issue of *Third Eye* and has published *Dragon Fire, Dancing Dogs and Dangling Dreams* (Northwoods Pr., 1978).

Rennis H. Sees writes: "I am now working on a series of nine tapestries. Nearing completion is an art history graph. I live to write and weave."

Ruby P. Shackleford (R.S.) has published six volumes of poetry: *Dreamer's Wine, A Visual Diary, Poems, Poems 4, Ascend the Hills,* and *The Bamboo Harp.*

C.A. Smith has appeared recently in *Dakotah Territory, The Mainstreeter, Purr, Pearl,* and *The Lunatic Fringe.* His most recent book is *New Songs From the Old Revolution* (Satyagraha Pr.)

Jared Smith, ex-member of the *New York Q* staff, has appeared in *Poet Lore, the NYQ, the Smith, Coe Rev., Partisan Rev., Bitterroot, Greenfield Rev.,* et al. His anthology, *Speak For The Silence: New Voices of the Long Poem* will be published by Dogsoldier Press (1978).

Laurel Speer has published in *Mississippi Rev., The Smith, Kansas Q., Texas Q., Remington Rev.,* et al. Her chapbook, "The Sitting Duck," was published by Ommation Press.

Gary Sterling writes: "My wife, the real secret of everything, dancer, choreographer, teacher (member of the Royal Academy of Dance, brag), singer, pianist, exquisite cook (her cheese cake! the world's best and only real spaghetti, but ah! my rabbit and souvlakla! but ah! her salads! but ah! my curries!....)"

Ronica Stern is an actress, teacher, lecturer, and writer. She lived in Greece for three years, completed a novel, and is working on a second.

Debrie Stevens is writing an "off-beat novel" and is putting together pamphlets of her poetry.

Nancy Stone runs a "small publishing venture," the New South Company, in California.

Robert Joe Stout's novel, *Miss Sally* (Bobbs-Merrill) appeared in 1974. His poetry chapbooks include "Trained Bears and Hoops" (1974), "Camping Out" (1976), "The Trick" (1976), and "Swallowing Dust" (1977).

John Thomas Stovall is a free-lance book reviewer for the *Chicago Tribune* and has appeared in the *DeKalb*

Literary Arts J., The Poet, The Archer, and *Voices International.*

Eileen Stratidakis' poems have appeared in the *South Carolina Rev., Cimarron Rev., Florida Q., The Wisconsin Rev., Apalachee Q., Aspect,* et al. She is on the staff of the *Georgia Q.*

Robert J. Svoboda, a Cleveland city planner, has appeared in *New Collage, Small Pond, Telephone,* and *WCLV Cleveland Guide.*

Melissa Szymanski has appeared in *Vega, The Poet, Bardic Echoes,* and *Circus Maximus.*

Marcella Taylor teaches creative writing in Minnesota and has published poems in about twenty literary mags and journals.

J. Maurice Thomas teaches creative writing and English in North Carolina.

Scott Thomas has appeared in *Pierian Spring, Touchstone,* and *Encore.*

June W. Thornton, a computer attendant, has appeared in the *DeKalb Literary Arts J., Pegasus,* and *The Biennial College Anthology.*

WDTimmerman writes: "I am a common laborer who wants to know no specialization, except in writing, photography, and in relating to the earth."

Marilyn Throne's poems have appeared in *Ball State Forum, Louisville Rev., Encore, Cape Rock* and *Lyrical Voices: An International Poetry Anthology.*

Rick Ulman writes, "I make things of notes and other things of words. I play a lot of instruments. One of them is the typewriter."

Charles Upton has published *Panic Grass* (City Lights Pocket Poet Series) and *Time Raid* (Four Seasons Foundation Writing Series, 1968).

David Vajda has appeared in *North Coast Poetry, Images,*

Green's Mag., Bitterroot, Third Eye, The Stone, The Small Pond, et al.

Lois V. Walker has appeared in *Miscellany, Hand Book, Dark Tower, The Small Pond, Measure,* et al. Her sculpture has shown at Womanart Gallery in Manhattan.

The Walrus (a.k.a. ?) is from Olney, TX.

David Wann writes: "My fondest aspiration is to become a truck farmer/writer." He is working on a novel, *Bailing Out.*

Robert R. Ward has appeared in *Mirror Northwest, Port Townsend J., Bitterroot, Pacific, Puget Sound Q., Huron Rev., Kansas Q., Transactions of the Pacific Circle,* et al.

Roger Weaver has appeared in *The Massachusetts Rev., The North American Rev., The Colorado Q, The Northwest Rev.,* et al. He is co-editor of *Aftermath* (Greenfield Rev. Pr.)

Randy Weinstein has published in *Outpost, Bardic Echoes, A Poem— A Vision Anthology,* and *The New Island Anthology for Poets.*

W. Blaine Wheeler writes: "In my travels I have noticed that people want to forget, to minimize, to disregard those times of loneliness which must occur to all. Rather than weakness, I find that strength can come from loneliness; therefore, I celebrate moments of loneliness in [my] poetry."

Robert F. Whisler has appeared in *The Apalachee Q., Canadian Author and Bookman, Georgia Rev., Green's Mag., The Lake Superior Rev., Texas Q.,* et al.

William M. White's book, *All Nature Is My Bride,* was a Book of the Month Club selection and he has "published poems in over 100 different quarterlies, reviews, and literary magazines."

Doris Wight has published a book, *Bird Wings* (Wayside Pr.) and "400-some poems in 130-some magazines and newspapers."

Kim Williamson's poetry has appeared in *Epoch, Green's Mag., Florida,* and *Windless Orchard.*

Robert L. Wilson has appeared in *Quintessence, Gryphon, Cyclotron, Hoosier Challenger, Scimitar and Song,* and *The Further Range.*

Liz Wrenn is editor of *Thunderstorms of Thought,* a student magazine, and has appeared in *Free Spirit* and *The Ed-U-Caster.*

Index To The Poems

A Christmas Hymn, 82
Addendum, 73
After the Storm, 86
After Work, 107
A Guidance Counsellor's
   Evening Prayer, 83
A Life, 59
A Miracle, 82
Annie Tackett, 61
A Prayer for all Mankind, 86
Asking Too Much This Time, 71
A Strong Dissolve, 90
At the Break of Day, 56
At the Shoreline, 89
Autumn, 84
Avoidance, 29
Aye, Good Sailor, Aye, 39
The Beast, 42
"The bridge," 59
Broken Commandments, 57
Calling Captain, Clive, 16
The Captured, 97
Come, And Spread the Sight!, 50
Communion With the Dead, 73
Conversing: 12, 63
Counterpoint, 107
Daughter At Ten, 17
Dawn, 84
December, 66
Descent, 46
Divine Destiny, 81
Divine Power, 76
Doves, 19
Drawn-Out Glue, 58
Drink It Down, 94
Earth's Rebirth, 79
Enigma, 68
Faith, 80
Fields, 41
5/1, 89
Flute Song, 36
For the End Times, 78
From the Nest, 24
Gallery, 91
Genuflections, 93
Georgia O'Keefe Paints, 88
Glancing in on a Brand-New High
   Rise Apartment for Elderly
   People, 92

Gravity, 18
Heather, 80
The Hermit Thrush, 47
Holding-Tank, 106
Illumination, 38
In Lent, 81
In Pursuit of Excellence, 85
Introductory Botany, 65
it was raining then, 37
Jaded Green, 55
Keeping Up With Weather &
   Politics, 20
The Knot, 70
Little Quickie, 69
Long Live the Hills,
   The Hills Are Gone, 54
"Manor" Beside Fiery
   "Brooks" of Hell, 27
Many Deaths, 53
Mason, Turk and Market, 49
Memory of a Family, 13
Morning Mine, 75
Mother, 51
Mother, 79
Musical Drains, 23
My Love's Ears, 91
Near the Subways, 64
Nesting, 105
Next Tuesday, 65
No. 260, 67
Notice, 93
NX211, 60
One Year Later, 96
On Paranoia, 98
Ordained Acts, 22
"Orpheus played silence
   in his song," 88
Peace, 76
Peaches of Hogback Hill, 100
Photographer/Clown, 108
The Plight of Youth, 85
Poem Thief, 99
Poetry Course, 32
The Pornography of Guilt, 95
Prayer, 64
Prayer of a Prodigal Son, 43
Quiet..., 15
resurrectionist, 26

Return, 40
"Ruby is going to marry a magician." 63
Shame, 41
Shotgun, 101
The Sign Is Down, 90
Small Desolations, 52
Snake Handler at the Fair, 34
Some People, 92
Sonata in Brown, for Woodwinds, 35
Sonnet VII, 28
Spring Outing, 74
Springtime in David Wann, 68
Spirits, 77
Star Gatherer, 7
Sternal, 38
Susan in Newcastle, 8
The Tattered Towel, 60
Terminate, 30
"The auction flyer said there were items", 14
Thoughts at a Concert, 62
Three Day Weekend, 48
Three Parts A Loneliness, 45
The Timid Author's Lament, 33
The Toad, 87
To An Only Son Newly Departed For College, 46
To A Nun/ standing on the shore, 23
To A Young Ballet Dancer, 21
To A Young Poet, 62
To Seven Canada Geese, 87
Underwater, 72
The Visit, 13
Voiceless, 44
We Came to Clean/ We Aim To, 103
What To Do, 74
"When I play tennis I don't think about it." 75
Why Don't You Feel Anything When I Touch You There, 31
Without Fear, 78
Yes, 105
your more, my less, 102